Praise for Previous Books

The Empty Notebook Interrogates Itself

"Quick, open these pages and meet *The Empty Notebook*—the enduring nothingness out of which all is generated, the negative capability on which artists thrive, ecstatic world-wanderer, canny literary imitator, driven self-obsessive—as vivaciously and audaciously imagined by Susan Thomas. Pleasures await."

—Jeanne Marie Beaumont

"Giacomo Leopardi, the great Italian poet, once wrote that great works of art, 'even when they give a perfect likeness of the nullity of things always serve as a consolation, rekindling enthusiasm.' That is precisely what Susan Thomas' incredibly original *Empty Notebook* poems do. By turns ironic, tragic, comic and filled with the paradoxical gusto of pathos, Thomas' poems shows us a way to start from nothing and claim everything. This is a major work in the tradition of Popa and Zbigniew Herbert whose landscape is the imagined world that mirrors, and, more, ironically completes our own."

—Richard Jackson

Among Angelic Orders

"These are stories in which the past permeates the present and in which memories have enough intensity to summon ghosts. Susan Thomas's graceful writing, particularly powerful in the first person, is filled with tender irony and heart."

—Joyce Johnson

ALSO BY SUSAN THOMAS

POETRY
State of Blessed Gluttony
The Empty Notebook Interrogates Itself
The Hand Waves Goodbye - chapbook
Voice of the Empty Notebook - chapbook

STORIES
Among Angelic Orders

TRANSLATIONS
Last Voyage: Selected Poems of Giovanni Pascoli,
with Richard Jackson and Deborah Brown

In the Sadness Museum

Susan Thomas

Fomite
Burlington, VT

Copyright 2017 © by Susan Thomas

Cover image: Copyright © Lynn Saville 2017

All rights reserved. No part of this book may be reproduced in any form or by any means without the prior written consent of the publisher, except in the case of brief quotations used in reviews and certain other noncommercial uses permitted by copyright law.

ISBN-13: 978-1-944388-28-7

Library of Congress Control Number: 2017949220

Fomite
58 Peru Street
Burlington, VT 05401
www.fomitepress.com

For Maeve and Willie this time—
bringers of joy and chaos.

And, as always, for Peter—
master of revelry and constant support.

Contents

I.	1
In Medias Res	3
Disaster	4
In the Sadness Museum	6
The Key to Solipsism	8
Now and Then	9
Perpetual Motion	10
Weather Update	12
Handicapped	13
Crash and Burn	14
Ode to Cappuccino	16
Two Bodies	17
The Messenger	18

II.   21

History of the Main Complaint   23

My Ecstasy   28

Dining Table with Two Ghosts   30

The Blue Window   31

Violent Still Life   33

Caravaggio in the Cathedral of St. John   34

Remains   35

Norman Bates' House On Museum Roof   37

Kiss of the Spider Woman   38

Self-Elegy   39

The Beautiful Cars   40

Aqua Alta   42

In the Rothko Room   43

III.   45

The Rose Marble Table   47
The Suicide Club   49
Black Macadam Over White Asphalt   51
Danse Macabre   52
Questions for Salamanders   54
At the Edge   55
The Grove   57
The Sugar Bush   58
This Week in Vermont   59
Mud Season   60
The Soul Trembles   62
My Afterlife   63
Instructions for a Journey to the Underworld   65

IV. 67

In the Village of My People 69

Nostalgia 70

9/11 72

River of Grief 73

Trees in January 74

Amsterdam Avenue Hangover 76

Ode to Gossip 79

Runaway Bay, 2010 81

At Sea 83

Dinner in the Branicki Palace 84

The Catastrophe 87

Bluster 89

End of Summer, 72nd Street 90

Notes 93

Acknowledgements

The author wishes to thank the following magazines in which many of these poems first appeared, sometimes in different forms and with different titles:

Arts and Letters: "The Key to Solipsism"
Cerise: "Dining Table with Two Ghosts"
CUTTHROAT: "My Afterlife", "Self-Elegy", "Questions for Salamanders" (under the title, "Ode to Salamanders"), "At the Edge" (under the title, " Sestina"), "Caravaggio in the Cathedral of St. John", "Aqua Alta", and "Norman Bates' House On Museum Roof"
Ellipsis: "Violent Still Life"
Indiana Review: "Runaway Bay"
Literal Latté: "Dinner in the Branicki Palace", "Danse Macabre"
MacGuffin: "Mud Season"
Manhattan Review: "Beautiful Cars"
MARGIE: "In Medias Res"
The Mississippi Review: "Instructions for a Journey to the Underworld", "History of the Main Complaint", "In the Sadness Museum" (MR Prize 2010)
Oberon: "End of Summer, 72nd Street", "Now and Then"
Poetry Miscellany: "Black Macadam Over White Asphalt"
St. Petersburg Review: "The Rose Marble Table", "Disaster"
The South Carolina Review: "Questions for Salamanders" (under the title, "Amphibious Passage")
The Same: "In the Village of My People"
Wings Press Anthology (The Heart's Many Doors): "Two Bodies"

I must also express my deep gratitude to Richard Jackson, Jeanne Marie Beaumont, and Jill Pralle for important suggestions and editorial advice, and my publishers, Marc Estrin and Donna Bister, for their responsive and enthusiastic support.

I have forgotten what I wanted to say.
The blind swallow flies back to her palace of shadows,
The empty boat sails up an arid estuary,
This night of frenzied absentmindedness.

    -Osip Mandelstam
    (Trans. James Green)

Whatever we say
we know there is another
language under this one

    -W.S. Merwin

In the Sadness Museum

I.

In Medias Res

Back from getting the paper
you notice the lock's been changed,
the furniture moved—the tweed sofa
turned black leather, the rocking chair
a hassock, the parakeet a hamster.
And the people who used to live here,
the family you used to know as
well as your fingers and toes?
Well—isn't this man in corduroy
at least familiar? Maybe so—or not—
have ten years passed? Things aren't
as they were. But a rhythm begins and
we dance, we eat what's on the plate,
go about our business pretending we
know what's going on in our head,
even though we know it isn't ours.
The shirt fits the man, the dance fits
the music even though it doesn't
move us. We go in and out the door,
raise the shade in the morning, shower
and anoint our strange bodies with
familiar lotions. The world spins around
itself, as do we, but something out there
far away needs to be acknowledged.

Disaster

Fiona calls from Paris to tell me
she got a call from Tokyo—
they just had a magnitude 9
earthquake that lasted four
minutes, and now they are
waiting for a tsunami to wipe
out some unsuspecting village
and maybe hit the west coast
of the U.S., or at least give
my kids a thrill in California
and Seattle. And isn't Seattle
on some giant fault like the one
in Chile that could go at any time?
But now I hear the tsunami has
already hit somewhere north
of Tokyo. No word yet of damage
and death, but how could they
get off unscathed? They can't.
And we can't. If it isn't earthquakes,
it's fire or terrorists, tornados,
or even a nuclear meltdown.
Aren't we all in some kind of danger,
waiting around for something to
happen? And meanwhile, we're

doing whatever we can to obsess
over things that can't really hurt us:
mortgages, taxes, tuition, apartments,
our next book, next trip, breakfast,
lunch, dinner. Nothing that phone
calls from Paris and TV news can't
disrupt, telling us it already happened,
and all of the demons and angels
that sit on the edge of our world, waiting
to drag us back into theirs, are watching
us, holding their breath, letting us fall
forwards or backwards, not knowing
which side is which and how we
got to wherever it is we are now.

In the Sadness Museum

We found the Saltines laughable,
the broken car door handle merely
inconvenient, the single earring
nostalgic. The curators tell us boxes
are intrinsically sad, but I always
find them exciting, containing a whiff
of something you always wished for.
I promised to send some artifacts
of my own sadness—my grandmother's
teeth, a wedding ring from a failed
marriage, the farewell note of a runaway
child, but then I thought perhaps they'd
prefer something exotic, like maybe
my friend's prosthetic arm that sticks
to the steering wheel whenever the weather
turns cold. I thought maybe they'd like
the 1949 Fleck Broiler that shorted out
my aunt's pacemaker. I wish I could send
them the flower bed, full of condoms
and cigarette butts, planted twenty years
ago by the owner of a now-defunct café
on 71st Street, which still sends up crocus
and daffodils every spring, but maybe I
should save that for the Museum of Hope

or the Survival Museum. Should I send
my rejection slips or the baby teeth I
collected before my children found my
stash, losing faith in both the tooth fairy
and me at the very same moment? Maybe
I could send them my favorite doll, headless
now, but how could I throw her away?
Do they want my son's favorite stretchsuit,
striped terrycloth, the knees worn out,
a vestigial elephant appliquéd on one side?
He's grown now with a child of his own,
but still I pine for the baby that filled
the suit. And of course, at last, there's
the artifact, me, so differently put together
than the original, so sadly asthmatic, itchy,
gray and puffy-eyed, so lumpy, weak-kneed,
often exhausted. And yet, still trying so hard
to be something I once imagined, so not really
hitting the mark, an odd little bundle of nerves
and enthusiasm, still idiotically hopeful, never
sad, never sad, but sometimes on the brink.

The Key to Solipsism

The picture is a model of reality.
The picture itself is a fact.
The world consists of fact.
In this picture, Naghma Mohammed,
a six-year old Afghan girl, who must
marry the son of a man who lent money
to her father, who borrowed it
to pay hospital costs for Naghma's
mother and funeral costs for the baby,
who froze to death because there was
not enough money for wood to heat
their tent. Because Naghma's father could
not pay back the loan with the money
he made teaching quails to sing and
selling them to other refugees in the camp,
he had to sell his daughter as collateral.
I have nothing to say about this picture.
I cannot answer, as Wittgenstein says,
that which makes no sense, but only
state its senselessness. We cannot think
what we cannot think. Therefore, we can
say nothing about that which we cannot
think about. And yet, I cannot stop thinking
about Naghma, or looking at her picture.

Now and Then

A paper lamp shaped like the moon
swings in a draft from the ceiling
and throws shadows across
the living room wall. Once
a small piano played forgotten
jazz when my father came home
late at night. Stars fall from the sky,
their bodies on fire, their tails
forgetting who they belonged to.
I laughed today but forgot
what I laughed at, like a dark
star whose life has imploded,
like a ruined piano whose keys
still remember chords played by
a hand that is no longer heard,
or a shadow still dancing in
a house that has fallen, house
and shadow remember that dance.

Perpetual Motion

We go away
        come back come clean
come around
        bring home the bacon
raise the children fall ill
        pass on pass away go to
our reward—because we cannot stop
        We run for office go to war
Winds blow in all directions
        Clouds burst tornadoes touch
down missiles rain bombs drop
        people explode
bodies fly apart
        The sky contains it all
the earth can't sit around
        clouds fly by while
stars come out and whirl around
        the heavens Everything
is going somewhere
        A terrible wind is screaming
We know it will
        tear us to pieces but we keep

on going wherever
        it blows us arms and legs
tangled together while
        everything under us melts.

Weather Update

The air's heavy breathing makes me sick,
keeps me up at night with its stench
of freezing sweat and shrieking whispers.
I hate the taste of the rain; it paws me all day.
I hate how the sky leers with its one dim eye

watching us trip the trick wires—
can't it see what we do to each other?
History's boobytrap opens and
bulldozers grind the luckless to dust,
while we slap at misfortune's hold.

My hands are screaming for a chance
to smack this week off the map
and you know next week won't be any better.
They're calling for flurries with suicide
bombers, torrential weeping into the night.

Handicapped
    NYC

Out of the dark night flies
        a wheelchair swathed in black plastic,
            swirling and sliding
    over the ice two days after the blizzard.

It races the drifted sidewalks,
        splashing through corner puddles
            while the rest of us shuffle through slush,
    babystep and wade through pools at the crosswalks.

The wheelchair speeds on, stopping at neatly
        bagged garbage sprawled at every corner,
            too far ahead for us to see
        if it stops to groom pathways

or hunt for thrown-out treasure.

Crash and Burn

If not for cosmic collisions
    where would we be now?
        Floating free in our appointed place

no rambunctious asteroids
    careening through the sky,
        pitching through roofs of houses like
    one in Nutley, New Jersey, where it fell
        into a bathroom, ruining newly-laid tiles

and no moon to drag the oceans up and down the beach

no tilting earth
    to give us nasty weather
        we complain about

and not even any us
    to nestle up among ourselves,
        creating more us to raise and send to school,
then move a thousand miles away,
    having more little us of their own (if we're lucky)

while we try not to think about the monsters
        we've become—we think birthday party,
what's-for-dinner, next election,
        not waterboard, Gitmo, stop-loss.

We tear hair out trying to save it all,
        we pray our science can rescue us—make fresh water
            out of the ocean, steal energy from the wind,

and avert the collisions that put us here on earth.

Ode to Cappuccino

Your dark body
draws me down
to the blinding world
of noisy toast,
forbidden butter, milk
whose surface rides
the cup like fair-weather
clouds on a bitter sea,
and beside it, newspaper
dark with disaster,
its white margins
frame a world I can't
swallow—I want to
drown in you, sweet bitter
cappuccino, your sugar,
sweetness of my own life,
from my flickering dreams
to dark morning news, I
drink your dying froth.

Two Bodies

My body stretches to pleasure,
reaching outward to
air, water, earth. I come
home in the murmur of stars
the pleasures of bed—rest, sleep, love.
My other body cringes, hiding
her eyes to the world. She penetrates
the heart, where her suffering is kept.
Does she wish an end to pain, hiding
her shame of useless days, endless
nights? She asks only
to still her raucous breath.

The Messenger

Your dreadful wings beat
the air, humming a song
I have always known
and has always sent me reeling.
Half angel/half serpent—
wings of skin and feather.
You hover. You perch.
You hesitate, then dive.

My pulse flutters and
falls, waiting for you
to dive down holding
the message you came
to deliver—whatever
hope or burden
you chose for me—
whatever it is, I take it
from you now and forever.

II.

History of the Main Complaint
   after the films of William Kentridge

1.

In Johannesburg, a man puts a coffee
cup to his ear and sees the world. I sit in
my kitchen in flowered pajamas, sipping
a coffee cup brimming with fear.
Kentridge has drawn the man naked—himself,
an artist—vulnerable, his fear and longing
exposed. He turns on the faucet and water fills
the room, rushes under the door into the street,
where people form lines, something in their eyes
like defiance. They are waiting for something
to happen. In the film, blood runs from the faucet
into the street where police shoot rifles into
the crowd. People are falling. Blood seeps from
their slowly-opening wounds. Blood fills the frame
while a black cat walks through the crowd like time
passing, as though history has already happened.
I sip my coffee waiting for an era to pass, the time
in which I counted, which came back to me
as a gift. Gifts can't be counted on; but once they
are received you think they are yours forever.

2.

A fat man in a business suit is sitting at a desk,
smoking cigars and answering telephones. His suit
is like armor. Nothing from the outside world
can touch him. I wait for my cell phone to bring
me bad news, I am wearing no armor, but cotton
pajamas to cover my heart. As each telephone
rings, the man in the film picks up the receiver.
He blows smoke into each mouthpiece. The cat,
history, sits on the desk of the man in the film
and he strokes it. I am waiting to outlive my own
history, the time I waited to come around again,
the time in which I knew how to matter. Kentridge
draws blue lines through the frame of the film,
connections that bisect the desk, the room,
the building, the street. The lines rise into the sky
where they become constellations resembling
the man who put the cup to his ear. The constellation
dissolves into home; veldt, barn, pond, rock,
utility tower. The man is back where his history started.

3.

The man in the business suit is eating
an enormous meal by himself. The table
in front of him, crowded with roasted
chickens, whole fish, fruit, vegetables,
is set with four glasses of wine. Outside
the building, a line of people shuffle
their feet and groan as their stomachs
rumble. My toast pops out of the toaster
and I scrape some butter over its surface.
The cell phone rings and I answer at once,
an appointment confirmed for later today.
The man in a suit drinks from all four glasses.
He eats the entire chicken, the fish, potatoes.
The line outside grows longer now, with more
rumbling of stomachs and cries for food.
The man in the suit devours some cake
and pie, then pulls a coffee press toward him.
Outside, there are even more people.
The coffee press rings and a handkerchief
in the man's pocket begins to weep. The man
in the suit rises from the table to feed the hungry.
He takes his empty plates to the window,
throws piles of bones down to the crowd.

4.

The naked man turns on a faucet, picks up
a razor to shave his face. The sink fills until
water spills over the floor, becomes an ocean.
The man in a suit sits on a chair at the edge
of the ocean, reading a newspaper. Children
and cows stand in the waves, but the cows
become carcasses and the children disappear,
as mine have, grown into shapes so different,
so changed from their childhood, as though
they had left at adolescence and never appeared
again. On Kentridge's beach he has drawn
cabanas with cows dancing inside them, with
light bulbs that spark and burst. Folded chairs
stand up on two legs to dance a tarantella
as once I sat waiting to dance, waiting for
my life to begin again and it did. In the film,
a light bulb drawn in the shape of a bomb
explodes into the street. Paper flies in every
direction, burying people whose blood soaks
the paper which covers the rock, the pond,
the field, the farm. I rise from the table to turn
on the faucet, wash dishes and vegetables
picked from the garden. The time ticks usefully

away—it fills itself with its own importance
as we wait for our own endings. Fear, longing,
defiance, action—are only minutes added
to history. Memory conquers fear, embracing
time with corrective lenses. The man who
held the cup rises from the pond to embrace
a woman who is naked except for her glasses.

My Ecstasy

I scavenge pleasure. Each day I track
the ecstatic. I pick up its scent on books,
on the clothing of passers-by, music that
travels the wind. I steal it, eavesdrop cell
phones in the street, idle waiting room chatter.

When syncopation grabs my feet, joy
dances me deep inside the music. Words
make me throb with delight while riding
the #5 bus down Broadway. Pavese thrills
me—I shiver and bounce in my seat reading

Popa's Little Box poems. I once found
the forest ecstatic—matching my pulse
to the pulse of things that held their silence
deep inside the earth. I wanted to be nameless,
breathless, I wanted to stand still to

keep my balance on the heaving forest floor.
But now I borrow from others what Maslow
called Peak Experience. Puccini, Balanchine,
music's sublimity, the relative nature of gravity—
And Matisse—who shows me how naked canvas

can mean more than painted surface when the
background describes the shape of the unsaid.
And how a blue skirt must be painted twenty times
until it tells the truth. And the ecstasy of nasturtiums
in a blue vase on a round table next to an open book.

Dining Table with Two Ghosts
after Bonnard

A substantial meal even for the living, but these
two pick at food like adolescents. Does the girlish
figure matter now? Especially when the tables
are turned and Renée, her suicide, years ago,
a wedding gift to M. and Mme. Bonnard, now
is the life of the party. Relationship has no legality
in death. She gleams like the striped satin tablecloth,
her blonde hair brilliant against it, her smile sharpens
the silverware, her eyes the luscious plums of every
still life Bonnard has ever painted. And Marthe,
as shadowed in life as she is in death, is used to being
a phantom, a camouflaged presence in every painting,
at every meal, like the Sumerian ghost who told his
friend that death was much like life only grayer. Maybe
it is only memory that shades or brightens, and now
Renée—released to Pierre's imagination by Marthe's
death—has taken her place at the center of the table.

The Blue Window
after Matisse

In this room I breathe blue.
Everything I hear is blue.
The vase smells blue
although it is green. Even
the red flowers in
the green vase are blue.

The blue roof of the house
outside the window beyond
the blue trees lifts blue
from the sky where even
white discs of clouds that
hover above us are blue.

What is bright can skid
to darkness. The sun's last
ray streaks green from the pale
horizon, summoning night and
its ravaged purple spikes. Fears
flake and peel, falling in darkness

to the moaning of stars in their
black cavern, until at last
the sun's random light returns
the density of blue to the sky
and relinquishes everything,
gives in to the gravity of blue.

Violent Still Life
after Van Gogh

How, then, could the flesh
of this apple remain calm, stop
its constant vibration? How could
it ever hold its center intact?
Only you could paint this way,
the haloed saintliness of fruit,
ready to levitate from the table,
the way you were always ready;
how could you ever stand still?
Your hand and feet could only
follow your frantic mind,
spinning beyond its boundaries—

unlike the stillness of this pear
beside the apple, never bursting
from its skin like these grapes,
which might fall to the floor or
might raise themselves to heaven
to meet whatever there is after we
separate from the essential stem
that holds us. This is how to paint
them. You paint as though you were
only here for a moment, trembling,
always on guard, ready to explode.

Caravaggio in the Cathedral of St. John
Valletta

In Malta, he paints the beheading of St. John the Baptist for the Knights Templar. He paints it brutal, real, no angels or marble columns. Just peasants committing a bestial act in an austere prison with indirect light and off-center subject. No one who sees it can look away from the simple peasant faces determined to perform a task they can't figure out. Their confusion is obvious, but something else has begun to darken their features.

He understands this, sees it when he looks in the mirror. He thinks the Knights will protect him because of the painting. Maybe it is the best work he has ever done. But the painting betrays him. It shows the guilt tightening his own features as it creeps across the faces of the peasants. Soon it will happen again—another bar fight, another murder, another run for his life. And this time the Knights know exactly who he is.

Remains

I wish I'd known Schopenhauer
back when I coasted on rickety skis
each day to visit the friendly wild
things that lived in our field and backwoods.
I was new to the uplands, learning
to track things in the snow, big things,
little things, paw prints,
feathers and scratchy claw marks,
curious who was there, who ran
and flew and skittered and leapt,
but all it was really about was who
was eating whom at what particular time.
One day, with animal tracks in front
of me that were large and deep, two
feet apart from front to back, then three,
then four. I suddenly knew the thrill
of something chasing something else
and the terror of what it was chasing.
I wish I'd known Schopenhauer.
I wouldn't have been so shocked.
I would have known there was evil
in the forest. Schopenhauer was right—
it's everywhere, everything, all inherently evil.
I tracked the long excited leaps of

whatever was chasing into the brambles.
There at the edge of the woods—fur,
blood, scent of horror, and then deeper
into the forest, the remains of a deer—
teeth, hooves, bones, viscera.
What I needed was Schopenhauer sitting
there on the page, muttering inherent evil,
malevolent volition, bellum omnium of eternal
predation, eternal becoming, endless flux.

Norman Bates' House On Museum Roof
NYC

We know the setup—Janet Leigh in the motel shower, Tony Perkins upstairs in the mansion, with the skeletal remains of his mother dressed and seated in a rocking chair. But, in Psycho, it's the basement that brings on the real horror. It's always about the basement, always what's underneath us. But here, on the roof of the Metropolitan Museum of Art, there's no basement below us. Downstairs is the museum's second floor with Van Gogh, Manet, Velasquesz clinging to the walls. Goya is just down the hallway, protecting us from evil and guiding us toward the Grand Staircase. But here, on the roof, there is only the façade of a red Gothic house. Something about it repels us but also draws us in. We fear it because we know it—an image Hitchcock has planted inside us. And, of course, we aren't alone on this roof. We share our fear with everyone else. We creep up to the house and laugh at ourselves as we look through the empty windows and into our mindless terror.

Kiss of the Spider Woman
Carkeek Park, WA

Did you see me reach in mid-air, my hand
grasping the rail of a staircase suspended in fog?
Descending cliffs to the beach of a bay, invisible
below me, a green splotch on my map. Staircase,
rail, grab for safety—I put down my hand to gasp
fire, vertigo, tightening throat. Did you see us dash
over the cliff to the car, spiral out of a backwards
skid, fumbling for Benadryl, *lucky, lucky*—three
still intact in the bowels of my purse, speeding
inland looking for traffic, horn honking, yelling:
hospital, hospital. Then, bed, needles, doctors,
nurses, bottles of ice slamming through veins,
fire in my face, my chest, and *lucky* rolled around
in my head, rolled off my tongue, *lucky*. Hours
and days and weeks spun past. My hands began
to unclench, found white silk to weave and knit,
crochet, even macramé. Patterns hang from windows,
walls and ceilings. I never go out anymore, but ask
my friends upstairs to see my handiwork. They never
leave. They've all moved into my apartment. I can
see them waving in the shadows with my medial eyes.
I wave back. I haven't bought groceries for weeks.

Self-Elegy

You will say I kissed strangers, gave
soup to passers-by. You will say I
moved slowly, dropped things. But
will anyone speak of my dreams?
I don't think I ever told them—ruined
landscapes, mutilated trees, children
sinking into the desert. Fish will cry
for me. Frogs will sing like demented
angels remembering snowstorms that
shot from my eyes. My fingers touched
fire, reached for constellations, swam
rivers. My ears heard forests colliding,
buildings collapsing, telephone voices
screaming good news/bad news. I have
won the sympathy of flowers—they
bloom then wither to show me how.
Fish weep for me though I have never
spoken my love of water, my fear of fire,
my obliterating dreams, which bleat their
terrible madness into someone else's
sleeping brain, some innocent among
pillows, to celebrate my unremembered life.

The Beautiful Cars
from Robert Frank's photograph
"Public Park, Ann Arbor, MI"

They lounge under the trees—
two-toned Buicks, Pontiacs,
Oldsmobiles, waxed and buffed
and simonized, they are glamorous,
like movie stars waiting for their
close up, holding still so nothing
will ruin their make-up. The cars
are watchful, smug, on guard
while they pose for the camera.
They are smitten with themselves,
with their chrome and their metallic
paint, their smiling bumpers and
their portholes like perfect smoke
rings running down their fenders.

The cars are vain and lazy. They prefer
to pose where they can be admired.
They dislike heavy feet mashing
their pedals. They shrink from sweaty
hands on their perfect steering wheels.
They are disdainful of the road where
they are expected to perform, to spin

their immaculate white-walled tires
to take greasy oil into their gleaming
engines. They are forced to obey
reductive road signs that trivialize
their every movement, that imply they
are machines that simply stop and go.

The beautiful cars don't like each other.
Some are jealous of the Buick's two-tone
paint job, the Pontiac's deco trim, the sexy
bedroom headlights of Oldsmobiles. They
spew each other with exhaust, drop their
mufflers, hurl curses concerning vulnerable
inner parts, make fun of rising numbers on
odometers, a widening radius of an aging
steering wheel, the sibilant shriek of brakes
that sport last season's shoes. Sometimes
they play tricks—remove gas pedals, lock
doors, siphon gas. The beautiful cars have
no mercy. They love the crazy zig-zag lindy
hop of a blowout, get a rush watching head-on
collisions. They aren't responsible for mishaps.
The beautiful cars are mean and hate their drivers.

Aqua Alta
Venice

The siren goes off at 5 AM. It blows us awake to the tapping of hammers, to the shouting of workers in the calle below, putting together platforms for us to walk on today to rise in the Aqua Alta, the high waters. Forget the Rialto market, the Tintoretto at the doge's palace. Forget the Accademia. Today only the Tiepelos make sense. Men, women, horses, deities of myth and religion, all swimming and flying and kicking their way to the ceilings of palaces, the heavenly domes of the churches. And of course, the Bellini Madonna in the Frari, if you can make your way through the Piazza. She is ascending to Heaven with angels to boost her. She rises above the Earth, above the air, above the waters, her face losing its years, losing its grief. Losing all earthly connection, she rises.

In the Rothko Room
Phillips Collection, Washington, D.C.

A perfect note of pure color
floats out from the surface
of each canvas to suffuse
the eyes, skin, blood and cells
of the onlooker, who is seated,
as Rothko instructed, on
a square bench in the middle
of the room. Her muffled heart
slows, drops a beat to absorb
the pigments. There is a second
way to see when only absence
is real. Memory persists, and
fear of what is left. What new
regrets and terrors may yet
arrive? And how to stand them?
But here the melted world peels
back, saturated with light, with
texture. Surface spills into deeper
realms of pulverized existence.
She breathes in color—orange,
burgundy, mauve, yellow—
exhales and disappears inside it.

III.

III

The Rose Marble Table

Remember how we sat in the garden,
the darkening sky, the darkening earth,
how three limes on the octagonal table
stood out in the darkening light,
how we talked until we couldn't see
the green leaves beneath our feet
nor the limes on the table,
the octagonal table, its surface
like skin slowly dying in the darkening
day, how we talked of a time when
you'd be gone and I'd sit all alone
in the garden in the dark
with the rose marble table
there in the deep shade of late
afternoon and your skin would be
as cold as the skin of the table,
its octagonal top reflecting the light
that is left at the end of the day,
its pedestal shaped like your arms
that can no longer hold me
up to the tree to reach for the limes
that grew there—limes that we
placed in a bowl on the rose marble table,
where we sat and palmed the green limes

to warm our cold hands until it was dark
and we passed from garden to house
where you lifted me into my bed
near the window and kissed me
goodnight and pulled down the shade
in the dark and I dreamed of
the garden until it was light every day.

For my Grandmother, Fannie Tomshinsky

The Suicide Club

There were five of us.
We met on Thursday afternoon
for ginger snap cookies and tea.
We told jokes and played the game
of Clue where all the wounds were
self-inflicted. Sometimes we talked
about imagining something we could
hang on to when the pain wrapped
around us. The jokes had punchlines
like: the knife, the rope, the medicine
cabinet. Most of us told no one else,
but sometimes I called Suicide Hotline
to ask if they knew a joke. It always
worked, even when they hung up
on me. Somehow it broke the mood.
Even the weather report could work.

I could think of tomorrow's weather—
rain, snow, even partly cloudy—
I could see the clouds forming,
cumulus, floccus, stratus—tumbling
across my brain. We never saw
each other outside, but sometimes
I brought my kids to hear Ray play

the organ for the Ebenezer Baptist Church
on Sunday mornings. It was fine to see
his small, beatific white face and red hair
bopping in a sea of shining black faces
and swaying, sequined gospel robes.

We met on Thursdays for years, except
one of us, a famous poet. In some dazzling
collapse of her vast imagination, she
went home one Thursday afternoon and
swallowed everything on her bathroom
shelf. But we still tried to believe—no,
I did—I believed. I believed in the way
the music made me feel, in Ray's happiness.
I believed we would be okay, would all
grow old. We'd only have to picture
something, feel something we never saw
or heard or felt before—like the organ
chords Ray struck or the notes the choir
held, or the joy on their faces, singing,
Walk Around Heaven All Day, no matter how
dark or cold everything and everyone else got.

Black Macadam Over White Asphalt

Maybe I'll die in New Jersey near the Hackensack
River, clutching a Jersey tomato or a Bischoff's
ice-cream cone like the ones I couldn't eat in
my youth fearing midriff bulge and popular
mean girls who sat at the counter. The sky
was always gray then, or maybe it was pollution.
I'll probably die in New Jersey, bored, waiting
for the No. 70 bus to pick me up on Rte. 4,
and it will most likely be Tuesday, the most boring
day of the week, even worse than Monday because
you expect the worst from Monday but it doesn't get
any better and by Wednesday you've gotten used to
the awfulness of New Jersey. Yeah, maybe I'll die
in New Jersey, the Bergen Evening Record
lying unread on my doorstep, pissed on by
my neighbor's cat, wishing I was someplace else.

Danse Macabre
Vermont

Again, the raccoons got it all, the corn,
        frilly and long-limbed, so full of silken
rattle in the sideways-shifting wind.
        I thought we'd struck a bargain with
the deer, offered them music to soothe
        their frazzled nerves, and epicurean compost,
coffee grounds, eggshells, vegetables,
        perfectly displayed on top of the pile,
unsullied by weeds and manure, tempting
        them to stand guard over the fenced-in corn,
scare smaller beasts away. But no, they crowded
        into their deer yard, dreaming orange rinds
and apples, blueberries still on the bush, varied
        cultivars of expensive tulip bulbs, freshly laid
in the ground for them to excavate at their leisure,
        never thinking of the field and their job as lookouts.

But of course, it's not like we have nothing else
        to eat, what with thousands of string beans born
each day when they should have died long ago,
        and artichokes that over-wintered when I forgot
to pull them up last fall, and squash, still pushing
        their way past appointed boundaries, swelling,
coloring, growing so big I can't even lift them

    to harvest, thanks to global warming. And
the corn. Each gap was perfectly filled with seed
    that slid from tassel to silk to cob and grew to
shining fullness, swollen in its husk and ready
    to pick. All this happened with the radio on
all night in the corn rows, playing Gershwin, Debussy,
    Poulenc, so as to not alarm the deer but suggest
a presence in the garden alert to all shenanigans.

I should have played something more aggressive,
    maybe Wagner or Beethoven or maybe
Shostakovich, at least that would have been
    fitting accompaniment to their marauding
presumption, each note a cue for the masked
    and wrathful raccoons. Of course I was wrong.
Seeing it in retrospect, with the eye of a director,
    this mistaken music was horribly mismatched
to their rough choreography. It must have induced
    some parody of adagio, a bestial dance
emphasizing clumsiness. Now I blame myself
    for their rampage, the loss my fault, my profound
misunderstanding of animal behavior. The price?
    The corn field, my treasure, crowning jewel of
my garden, trashed and mauled and bitten to pieces.

Questions for Salamanders

In the pond you long for trees
and moss to rest your weary
skins on. On a stump do you dream
your flesh becomes liquid, deep as
a river? Do you ride your bones
like passengers sailing to the next
world without a qualm, trusting
your destination, trusting the breeze
that blows you?

                Or do you flail
in tall grass hissing in amphibious
tongues at the other inhabitants
of rock, tree, dirt? Do you loathe
and envy the fish, the frog, and even
the skittering waterbug on the pond's
still face while you must creep
over every twig and leaf
in a world you never chose?

At the Edge
    after Edvard Munch

Young girls in a storm at the edge of the sea
in their evening clothes and their naked feet,
behind them the house, its windows screaming,
shakes in the oncoming storm's semi-darkness.
In the house, mothers and fathers, uncles and aunts,
wonder what time the young girls will return.

Why should they wonder if the girls will return—
they can't stand forever at the edge of the sea.
Inside, they are drinking, the uncles and aunts.
They see girls swaying on cold, sobbing feet.
In the sparks of oncoming darkness,
the windows of all the houses are blazing.

The houses are cold, the windows are screaming.
Inside, who wonders which girls will return?
They flare in the storm's almost darkness,
each girl ablaze at the edge of a sea,
evening clothes trembling above throbbing feet.
Inside the house, aunts and mothers are drinking.

Mothers and fathers, they drink and they stare
while inside the room, windows are screaming
at young girls in their gowns and bare feet.

They call out to the girls who will never return,
who scream at the storm at the edge of the sea,
their anger ablaze in the comforting darkness.

Glasses and windows, in the storm's darkness
rage at fathers and uncles, not mothers or aunts,
who stare at the girls stepping into the sea.
Before them, curtainless windows are shrieking.
They call to the girls who will never return,
terrified girls in their gowns and bare feet.

Young girls in evening gowns and bare feet,
their eyes flash in the storm's early darkness,
cry out through the storm they will not return
to a house of mothers and fathers, uncles and aunts
who don't speak of girls, only drinks and their dinner.
So the girls, the young girls, disappear in the sea.

In the sea, their clothes sink under blue feet.
Girls silently screaming in deep water darkness
while their mothers and fathers drown in their cocktails.

The Grove

From pain's broken back
grow cypresses—trees of despair,
their unhappy limbs reaching
upward into emptiness.

Pain shuts its eyes to a world
that keeps spinning
without a pause for agony.

Why won't it let us
die, not once, not twice—
but constantly, while we follow grief
to where the trees stop growing?

The Sugar Bush

Blue tubes tether maples
and draw away their sap
like arteries from a human heart,
like tubes around a patient.
Dead leaves line the sugar bush—
we crunch them underfoot
in our greedy lust for sugar.

Death is all around us—
dead leaves, dead limbs,
our well-loved friends and family
who couldn't wait for Spring.
The trees reach out to us,
leaves resembling hands
that wave to us from the future.

This Week in Vermont

Last week was string beans and okra, artichokes, tomatoes, hot sun shrieking all day. At night, stars sprinkled the sky and the Milky Way haloed the rooftop but we never noticed. We were watching the news on TV. Candidates, crashes, cities in ruckus. But this week we had storms everyday. Lightning struck everywhere—no lights, no water, phone or TV. Absolute silence after the storm—and outside, when we went to watch the sky clear, Northern Lights careened in the sky.

Mud Season
Vermont

Redbud, willow, cherry blossoms—
someone else's spring. Here
we've got snow squalls flowering
in the meadows. Drifting snow
blooming in the window, icicles
growing from the roof. Sleeping
bears aren't up yet, but beavers
and raccoons are. You can see
their footprints sprouting at
the edge of ponds and lodges.

We have two seasons of dying—
one for those who can't face
winter, one for those who can't
hold on till spring. Our neighbor
died last week, a young musician.
His little girl sits at the piano
every day now, playing what
she thinks is jazz. Her father
told her she could make music
if she heard it in her head and
let her fingers dance.

Soon the woods will come alive
with crackling. Worms will tunnel
the thaw, pushing up dead leaves
to find each other in the dark, wiggle
their way to the surface. Under snow
drifts, tree roots will sprout, shove

their way through frozen ground
to keep their branches growing.
Snow drops are growing in melted
spots that circle trees. They shake
their heads, hanging onto their stems
for dear life in the weeping wind.

The Soul Trembles

Terrified of solitude,
frightened of the sky,
the soul cringes
in the open air.
Its body breaks to pieces
that fall to the floor.
While the soul sweeps up,
its heart clutching dust,
it pounds the air
with molecules, in and out,
covering every surface
but never adding mass.
Everything around us.
everything inside us.
Can the soul see
what we are made of?

My Afterlife

In the underworld I meet
my old boyfriends. Every one
of them wants a piece of me—
one to marry me, one to break
up again, but this time get me
to cry, another one insists we
had an unbreakable bond,
another just wants closure,
whatever that is. I tell them
all to hide and I will find
them, one by one, to free
them from my alleged spell.

Charlie, as usual, hides in
his room, feeling sorry for
himself and Joe goes off to
the dogs and Bob, never one
to mourn the past, forgets I'm
looking for him and marries
someone else—again. Michael
makes a nuisance of himself
and gets kicked out of the
afterlife and that takes care
of all of them except my two

husbands. So I find Joel and divorce
him, immediately this time. Then
I find Peter hiding in plain sight
but completely invisible to

anyone's eye but mine. He
comes when beckoned and
snuggles into the bed we
occupy in the afterlife, with
endless supply of crunchy
snacks, books, seltzer, tissues.

Instructions for a Journey to the Underworld

Wear sneakers. Stuff a pocket with tissues and treats for the dog. Fill the other pocket with coins; the ferryman won't accept your Easypass. Turn off your cell phone. Do not annoy the guards and don't take the same path twice. Bring a guidebook, compass, and map. But when you think you are lost, you are lost. Someone may find you but it may not be anyone you are happy to see. Don't complain. Be polite. Emulate Dante. Do not form attachments or make enemies. When invited anywhere, pretend you can't understand whatever language the invitation is issued in. The hills are steep but the flats are boring. The soil composition is so alkaline, it can put you to sleep. Resist the urge. Now is the time to drink the coffee. Don't take Valium, no matter how nervous this journey makes you. When told to leave, go. Do not wait for a signal or someone to see you out. Do not feel you must say goodbye. When the door slams behind you, let it. Don't look back.

IV.

VI

In the Village of My People
Lithuania

The old women lay flowers
on invisible graves whose
stones have been taken
for government buildings,

whose bones are silent
and forget their thickness,
the weight of their laughter.

The thud of the moon
falls onto our voices
that try to say what
our ears will not hear.
Who can forgive our
mouths for not speaking?

The silence we swallow
flies ear to ear
like a rumor careening
among the dead and dying stars.

Nostalgia
Paris

      Years ago
we used to stay
      in a rundown hotel
on the rue St. Benoit.

      Every night
we came home from cafés
      at St. Germain des Prés—or from
the Metro, after nights at

      African tango palaces
or Gypsy clubs near République.
      We were always tired, a little drunk,
so we took a shortcut

      through a street we called the Rue de Merde,
where old ladies in their nightgowns
      walked their dogs late at night.
We tried to avoid them in the dark,

      like people leaving the Belle Équipe or the Bataclan
last week. Only they weren't laughing or sauntering
      down the rue Jean-Pierre Timbaud.
They were screaming, crying, running, falling—

       those who could escape. They were avoiding
bullets and corpses. Watching them on the news,
       we longed for the quiet nights of old ladies
and their poodles, committing silent acts

of public indiscretion on the innocent streets of Paris.

9/11
NYC

Downtown, a stiff breeze blows
the heavy clouds across the river
with the passing rain. Uptown

we remember the day, go about
riding the subway or waiting
for the bus, grateful for

the change in weather despite
a scent of future bombs
hanging in the air.

River of Grief
Newtown, CT

The children are rising in the river—
their crayons, their mittens, their lost
teeth and light-up velcro sneakers,
their winter hats that make them look
like penguins or kittens or angry birds,
their socks and other remnants of clothing,
all rising to the surface in the River.
Their parents are sinking to the bottom
with their brothers and sisters, their cousins,
their grandpas and grandmas, their teachers.
The rest of us float in the water.
We are all swimmers in the River of Grief.
We bump into picture books, legos, and
backpacks in the murk of the River.
We can't avoid getting soaked. We can't
breach the current or offer up solace.
We just keep our heads up and
try not to drown in the River of Grief.

Trees in January
NYC

Little ones with their arms outstretched,
big ones bound with twine and wire.
Their sweet stench fills the street,
and people avert their eyes while
dogs relieve themselves on the branches.
Last month they lined the sidewalks,
upright, gleaming, festooned with lights,
like chorus girls on a gaudy stage,
the air around them so fresh it made
me dizzy to breathe it. Last month our
bedroom window looked out on a forest
of trees instead of a 24-hour drug store.
We dreamed of the north woods, of what
we'd left behind us, and I walked through
them every day, invisible, feeling my breath
with their breath, touching their still-living
needles, groundwater still running
in their veins. But the sidewalks had
nothing for them, no life could flow up
the lopped legs, bodies severed from roots
that push through the living soil, made up
of things that gave themselves for others
to sprout, grow, give in and sacrifice their
lives in turn to keep the forest humming

with the pulse of every unnoticed, unnamed
insect, leaf, rock, squirrel. I have touched it
with my eyes. I remember its wordless song.
But these trees on the sidewalk refused
to hum, drowned out by piped-in carols,
their silence a warning.

Amsterdam Avenue Hangover
NYC

Our neighborhood homeless Vietnam vet
who lives in the doorway of a boarded-up
restaurant on the first floor of our building,
flicks his still-lit butt in an arc that barely
clears the top of our heads—this morning
I handed him a coffee and he tossed it over
his shoulder, cursing, and calling me kike.
But sometimes he thanks me, his voice
so full of brotherly feeling I take a chance
every day on his mood— although now we ignore
him to stagger down Amsterdam Avenue
after the worst poetry reading ever, in which
the participating poets were pitted against
the regulars of a local bar that we rent Friday
nights for readings and the regulars sat on
the stools next to the mic, belching and farting
and telling dirty jokes in hissing whispers
that carried to the back of the room, or passed
back and forth in front of the mic while
announcing to themselves how much they
really had to go to the can and describing
their bodily needs while a guy near the podium
muttered constantly about the favor Hitler could
have done for them all and I tried to read my

Lithuanian ghost poem, which is usually a crowd
pleaser, but tonight only fodder for drunken anti-
semitic remarks that made me feel like I had chosen
the wrong profession and possibly the wrong life
but instead we choose Malachy's Bar and Grill
on Amsterdam Avenue for yet another random beer
on draft and another random stop at another Famous
Original Ray's for a slice of random pizza and find
ourselves out on the street ready to be sick or maybe
to fall under the wheels of a #7 bus or maybe crash
into the umpteenth stretch limo to pull up to the curb
in fifteen minutes and I think of my end—o, solitary soul—
am I really ready to lose it all on ill will, disgust,
mediocre poetry, indifferent pizza and bad beer, but
instead walk over to Columbus and the Emerald Isle
for possible salvation in Irish whiskey, and when
the bartender calls for last orders, pours us each
a Jameson's and hoists onto the bar a tiny old man
who blinks, takes a breath, and sings Danny Boy,
tearing up and wiping his eyes as the bar goes still
until the song is over and the man allows himself
to be lifted down from the counter and escorted
to the door by the barmaid, who watches him leave,
then tells the last of the crowd he's all right home

now—waited for the wee man to cross the street—
then we shuffle out, speechless and stand waiting at
the corner for the tiny dotted man on the light to
appear so that each of us can go our separate way
home—to bed, clean sheets, soap and water, books
on the nightstand and a lamp to read by whenever
we need whatever we need in their pages that gives us
our separate sustenance and keeps our separate peace.

Ode to Gossip
Vermont

I'm all ears for you—
dear gossip, you are gospel and glue,
rocking us in your dangerous currents,
floating us in your river of prattle,
news of now, news of then, and even
what's to come—rebirth perhaps or
maybe just dirt. Who knows?
I used to be up on all of it.

Where so-and-so was having dinner,
what tomatoes from whose garden,
followed by which parts of someone's
cow, raised solely on grass and grain,
no fodder in the mix, whose children
were winning which awards for what
activities and how the families were

planning their next vacation to
storm-ravaged third-world countries
to help construct sustainable housing
for displaced mudslide victims to
coincide with the grueling summer
practice for the above-mentioned activities.

I said I'd only listen to tales of
who was sleeping with whom, but got stories
instead of serious deprivation—wives,
husbands, even neglected illicit lovers—
no one was getting any. No murmurs of
spicy satisfaction were oozing under the door
and into the ear with alarming ease,
then sliding from ear to tongue to leave
a tingling sensation and no aftertaste.

Runaway Bay, 2010
   Jamaica

There weren't any limes this year, and hardly
any coconuts. This year on the beach
they had giant amps with heart-stopping bass,
and no one could dance to the new Jamaican music,
not even the Jamaicans. There were mysteries
this year: were those almonds dropping
from the tree to the roof? And were those rat bats
in the almond trees? Or were there people
in the yard, screaming like rat bats, tossing almonds
onto the roof?

                    This year we locked doors,
had no visits from Rasta Cliff with his excellent home-grown
herb. All the children were older, none of them ours,
no longer amusing as they grabbed food before grown-ups
came to the table. The latest baby had fewer smiles
than screeches and a creepy way of sticking out her tongue.
The ruthless sun hardly ever let up and I slathered
on sunblock to walk the beach at sunset with the gleeful leaping
Jamaican children and the young Jamaican couples
fucking softly in the waves. More of them this year and none of them
as quiet as they'd been the years before.

　　　　　We hardly spoke this year and when
we did I tried not to say what I wanted to say and you were relieved
when I managed not to say it. The morning swim
and the evening swim were lucky breaks in days that wouldn't end
until a storm slanted wind and rain through the slats
of our house on the beach and waves leapt up to rush under the door,
floating suitcases into the kitchen. I splashed
to the bathroom—*SHH, quiet*, you whispered, rolling over in bed.
Your voice broke up in the wind, rushed into the surf
that pushed everything up to our door—the towels and shoes and condoms
and wood left behind on the beach that day.
Shh washed out and *shh* washed back into the house like a wave.

At Sea
Adriatic

The rain won't stop. Drizzle. Torrent. Steady slant. It makes every place the same mess of cold, wet, slippery mush. The coffee is bad. Or is it tea? And just like the soup. We drink it anyway, to keep warm. And as we drink, we start to look the same. We are smaller, greyer, long noses shortening, small eyes growing wider. We are all sprouting eyeglasses. The passengers murmur in a moist, quavery monotone. Sky, water, horizon, coffee, tea, soup, passengers. All through the same damp, grey filter.

Dinner in the Branicki Palace
Poland

We stroll under beech trees,
all elegance and pleasure,
our fat babies in their lacy
bonnets, their fancy prams
just the same as Polish babies.
The Polish men in gabardine
suits tip their hats to us as we
promenade. We nod our heads,
slightly smiling. It is summer,
1935, in Warsaw. We are in
the first frame of a film they
show us in Poland. We are
tourists in the homeland now,
eighty years later, in the
reconstructed palace of what
they now call Old Town.

A bomb falls from the sky.
It drops down slowly toward
us, the audience squirming in
our seats. The bomb explodes,
the city in ruins, the faces—
they are our faces—terrified,
emaciated, the fat babies starving

and listless. We are herded into
the Ghetto, pushed onto the trains.
The city burns, bridges fall, and
in another frame, people return
by boat, ordinary people with
pickaxes, shovels. They dig
in rubble to rebuild the city.

We go to Bialystok and are given
a banquet at the Branicki Palace,
where no Jew was ever admitted.
We are toasted in the local bison
grass vodka, serenaded by a klezmer
band, who even managed a song in
Yiddish. When the band stops playing,
the bass player approaches.
Will I send him a bialy from New
York he asks? The roll will be stale.
No matter, he says, it's a relic
of the time when our town
was prosperous. There were Jews
who filled the public square, who
sold bialys in the central market.

I am astonished by this nostalgia
for the Jews. Half of me thrills
with ironic pleasure. The other is
skeptical and bitter. The band begins
to play again. I dance a little mazurka
on my way to the bathroom. A Polish
engineer sees me and jumps out of
his chair. Let's all dance! The hora
starts, and the Poles pull the Jews
from their seats, holding hands in
a circle, kicking up their feet, as if
we were in another age, as if we
were only dancing around the ballroom,
as if we were only out of breath.

The Catastrophe
    NYC

    1.

It happened at night.
    Everyone knew right away,
        except the early sleepers.

First there were screams
    from all the apartments—
        then silence—
the streets, the buildings,
    the absence of traffic.

Then stars fell out of the sky,
    landing, one by one,
        hissing on the sidewalk.
    The fat moon leered down at us, smirking.

    2.

When day came the sun gave
    more pain than light. We stumbled
        into each other, embracing.

Murmured *Terrible, terrible.*

Some people said—*It's like the other time,
    when the towers came down.*

    3.

No one could sleep.
    We went into the streets,
        grieving, shouting our outrage.

We were on the news,
    along with every detail
        of the catastrophe
and how it continued
    to unravel our lives.

Traffic snarled.
    Buildings had lights on all night.
        The stars still
    sprawled on the sidewalks,
        losing their light and whimpering.

    The moon shook its fist.

Bluster
NYC

We huddle at the bus stop against the tunnel of wind that explodes from the river and grabs at us around the towers. We're bundled in coats and scarves and hats, too wrapped up to meet each other's eyes. We're too swaddled to talk until the bus arrives and we start shedding pieces in the heat. We talk, we laugh, we sneer, and try to keep our tempers but we can't stop complaining of twisted characters, hideous speeches, terrible tweets, and even—treason. What will we do now? Because all of us are helpless and almost glad to bundle up, get off the bus and hit the wind.

End of Summer, 72nd Street
NYC

Sweat pours down the gutters,
   the sidewalks spark and prickle—
     on the corner
at a fruit stand,
   plums burst from their skins,
     and uptown, someone we

love is dying. The crosstown bus sobs
   under our window, passengers
     gasping in outside air, wringing
it out like a filthy handkerchief, cross
   streets as though
     they're wading in grief.

We cross the street too, skirting
   shadows cast by tall buildings.
     Inside the bank's dead air,
I hug your arm to keep warm. Outside,
   melons are exploding at the corner
     fruit stand. Grapes let go of stems,

drop at shoppers' feet, staring like eyeballs.
   We buy rolls and fruit and pastry, stop
     uptown at Barney Greengrass

for smoked fish our friend would eat if he
   weren't dying. At his bedside we ask
      him a question. He tries to answer,

he says he knows the answer, he'd tell us
   if he could, but he can't remember
      the words.
Back downtown, we stop
   to get dinner—the neighborhood
      is exhausted in the sinking sun.

Two guys with horns set up in front
   of the deli and they're blowing
      Harlem Nocturne all down the block.
Sweet jazz slides under the doorways like
   a westbound breeze from the river, heaves under
      the asphalt, wrenches joy from the sidewalk.

Passers-by throw coins in a hat, then dollars, then fivers.
   Cement shudders with delight, with dancers,
      with be-bop. The deli counterman comes out
with seltzers and knishes, throws a dollar in the hat,
   goes back inside, whistling. We put down our packages,
      grab each other, jitterbug, shake the pavement up.

Notes

Several years ago at an AWP conference, I encountered a travelling installation called *The Sadness Museum* by Buckbee, a Writer, Incorporated (who may or may not be fictional). My visit to *The Sadness Museum* and its photographs of objects that represented sadness to its contributors suggested my poem of that name.

"The Rose Marble Table" is a painting by Henri Matisse in the Museum of Modern Art, New York.

"At the Edge" is from the painting "The Storm" by Edvard Munch at the Museum of Modern Art, New York.

The Rothko Room is part of the Phillips Collection in Washington, D.C.

"Black Macadam Over White Asphalt" is after Cesar Vallejo's poem, "Black Stone Over a White Stone."

"Orpheus and Eurydice" is from a ballet by the same name by Pina Bausch.

"Two Bodies", "The Messenger", "The Grove", "The Sugar Bush" and "The Soul Trembles" are double ekphrastic poems from Metka Krasovich's illustrations of Emily Dickinson poems.

"History of the Main Complaint" uses portions of South African artist William Kentridge's film, History of the Main Complaint (1996).

"Norman Bates' House on Museum Roof" is taken from Cornelia Parker's 2016 installation, Transitional Object (PyschoBarn), on the roof of The Metropolitan Museum of Art. The installation references Alfred Hitchcock's 1960 film Psycho.

"Kiss of the Spider Woman" takes its title from Argentinian writer Manuel Puig's novel (El Beso de la Mujer Araña), published by Vintage, 1975.

"The Beautiful Cars" is from Robert Frank's photograph, *Public Park,* Ann Arbor, MI—from his book The Americans, published in France, 1958, by Robert Delpine, and in U.S., 1959.

Susan Thomas has published two previous collections of poetry, *State of Blessed Gluttony* (Red Hen Press, 2004) and *The Emtpy Notebook Interrogates Itself* (Fomite Press, 2011). She has also published two chapbooks, a collection of short stories, *Among Angelic Orders* (Fomite Press (2014) and is co-translator of *Last Voyage*, a collection of Giovanni Pascoli's selected poems (Red Hen Press, 2010). She lives in New York and Vermont with her husband, Peter Sills.

Fomite

About Fomite

A fomite is a medium capable of transmitting infectious organisms from one individual to another.

"The activity of art is based on the capacity of people to be infected by the feelings of others." Tolstoy, *What Is Art?*

Writing a review on Amazon, Good Reads, Shelfari, Library Thing or other social media sites for readers will help the progress of independent publishing. To submit a review, go to the book page on any of the sites and follow the links for reviews. Books from independent presses rely on reader to reader communications.

For more information or to order any of our books, visit
http://www.fomitepress.com/FOMITE/Our_Books.html

More Titles from Fomite...

Novels
Joshua Amses — *During This, Our Nadir*
Joshua Amses — *Raven or Crow*
Joshua Amses — *The Moment Before an Injury*
Jaysinh Birjepatel — *The Good Muslim of Jackson Heights*
Jaysinh Birjepatel — *Nothing Beside Remains*
David Brizer — *Victor Rand*
Paula Closson Buck — *Summer on the Cold War Planet*
Roger Coleman — *Skywreck Afternoons*
Marc Estrin — *Hyde*
Marc Estrin — *Kafka's Roach*
Marc Estrin — *Speckled Vanitie*
Zdravka Evtimova — *In the Town of Joy and Peace*
Zdravka Evtimova — *Sinfonia Bulgarica*
Daniel Forbes — *Derail This Train Wreck*
Greg Guma — *Dons of Time*

Fomite

Richard Hawley — *The Three Lives of Jonathan Force*
Lamar Herrin — *Father Figure*
Ron Jacobs — *All the Sinners Saints*
Ron Jacobs — *Short Order Frame Up*
Ron Jacobs — *The Co-conspirator's Tale*
Scott Archer Jones — *A Rising Tide of People Swept Away*
Maggie Kast — *A Free Unsullied Land*
Darrell Kastin — *Shadowboxing with Bukowski*
Coleen Kearon — *Feminist on Fire*
Coleen Kearon — *#triggerwarning*
Jan Englis Leary — *Thicker Than Blood*
Diane Lefer — *Confessions of a Carnivore*
Rob Lenihan — *Born Speaking Lies*
Colin Mitchell — *Roadman*
Ilan Mochari — *Zinsky the Obscure*
Gregory Papadoyiannis — *The Baby Jazz*
Andy Potok — *My Father's Keeper*
Robert Rosenberg — *Isles of the Blind*
Fred Russell — *Rafi's World*
Ron Savage — *Voyeur in Tangier*
David Schein — *The Adoption*
Lynn Sloan — *Principles of Navigation*
L.E. Smith — *The Consequence of Gesture*
L.E. Smith — *Travers' Inferno*
Bob Sommer — *A Great Fullness*
Tom Walker — *A Day in the Life*
Susan V. Weiss — *My God, What Have We Done?*
Peter M. Wheelwright — *As It Is On Earth*
Suzie Wizowaty — *The Return of Jason Green*

Poetry
Antonello Borra — *Alfabestiario*
Antonello Borra — *AlphaBetaBestiaro*
James Connolly — *Picking Up the Bodies*
Greg Delanty — *Loosestrife*
Mason Drukman — *Drawing on Life*

Fomite

J. C. Ellefson — *Foreign Tales of Exemplum and Woe*
Anna Faktorovich — *Improvisational Arguments*
Barry Goldensohn — *Snake in the Spine, Wolf in the Heart*
Barry Goldensohn — *The Hundred Yard Dash Man*
Barry Goldensohn — *The Listener Aspires to the Condition of Music*
R. L. Green When — *You Remember Deir Yassin*
Kate Magill — *Roadworthy Creature, Roadworthy Craft*
Tony Magistrale — *Entanglements*
Sherry Olson — *Four-Way Stop*
Andreas Nolte — *Mascha: The Poems of Mascha Kaléko*
Janice Miller Potter — *Meanwell*
Joseph D. Reich — *Connecting the Dots to Shangrila*
Joseph D. Reich — *The Hole That Runs Through Utopia*
Joseph D. Reich — *The Housing Market*
Joseph D. Reich — *The Derivation of Cowboys and Indians*
Kennet Rosen and Richard Wilson — *Gomorrah*
Fred Rosnblum — *Vietnumb*
David Schein — *My Murder and Other Local News*
Scott T. Starbuck — *Industrial O*
Scott T. Starbuck — *Hawk on Wire*
Seth Steinzor — *Among the Lost*
Seth Steinzor — *To Join the Lost*
Susan Thomas — *The Empty Notebook Interrogates Itself*
Paolo Valesio and Todd Portnowitz — *Midnight in Spoleto*
Sharon Webster — *Everyone Lives Here*
Tony Whedon — *The Tres Riches Heures*
Tony Whedon — *The Falkland Quartet*

Stories

Jay Boyer — *Flight*
Michael Cocchiarale — *Still Time*
Neil Connelly — *In the Wake of Our Vows*
Catherine Zobal Dent — *Unfinished Stories of Girls*
Zdravka Evtimova — *Carts and Other Stories*
John Michael Flynn — *Off to the Next Wherever*
Elizabeth Genovise — *Where There Are Two or More*

Fomite

Andrei Guriuanu — *Body of Work*
Derek Furr — *Semitones*
Derek Furr — *Suite for Three Voices*
Zeke Jarvis — *In A Family Way*
Marjorie Maddox — *What She Was Saying*
William Marquess — *Boom-shacka-lacka*
Gary Miller — *Museum of the Americas*
Jennifer Anne Moses — *Visiting Hours*
Peter Nash — *Parsimony*
Martin Ott — *Interrogations*
Jack Pulaski — *Love's Labours*
Charles Rafferty — *Saturday Night at Magellan's*
Kathryn Roberts — *Companion Plants*
Ron Savage — *What We Do For Love*
L.E. Smith — *Views Cost Extra*
Caitlin Hamilton Summie — *To Lay To Rest Our Ghosts*
Susan Thomas — *Among Angelic Orders*
Tom Walker — *Signed Confessions*
Silas Dent Zobal — *The Inconvenience of the Wings*

Odd Birds
Micheal Breiner — *the way none of this happened*
David Ross Gunn — *Cautionary Chronicles*
Gail Holst-Warhaft — *The Fall of Athens*
Roger Leboitz — *A Guide to the Western Slopes and the Outlying Area*
dug Nap— *Artsy Fartsy*
Delia Bell Robinson — *A Shirtwaist Story*
Peter Schumann — *Planet Kasper, Volumes One and Two*
Peter Schumann — *Bread & Sentences*
Peter Schumann — *Faust 3*
Peter Schumann — *We*

Plays
Stephen Goldberg — *Screwed and Other Plays*
Michele Markarian — *Unborn Children of America*

www.ingramcontent.com/pod-product-compliance
Lightning Source LLC
Chambersburg PA
CBHW021443080526
44588CB00009B/658